A WAVE
CALLED GRIEF

A WAVE CALLED GRIEF

by

WHITNEY POPA

designed & illustrated by
AnnaMarie Salai

OUR WEST PRESS

A Wave Called Grief copyright © 2024 by Our West Press

Cover design, illustrations, and layout design by AnnaMarie Salai, copyright © 2024 by West Finch, LLC.

Printed in the United States of America. All rights reserved, including the right of reproduction in whole or in part, in any form (except in the context of reviews). Please contact howdy@ourwestpress.com and hello@westfinch.com for written permission for other uses.

ISBN: 979-8-218-38161-5

ourwestpress.com // westfinch.com

*To my dad, who told me to
never lose my writing.
And to all of us figuring out
how to ride the waves.*

Whitney Popa

She woke up to a wave
crashing into her bedroom.

A Wave Called Grief

She rubbed the sleep from her eyes,
blinked hard,
and put her hand out to stop it.

It swept right over her,
pushing her onto her bed.

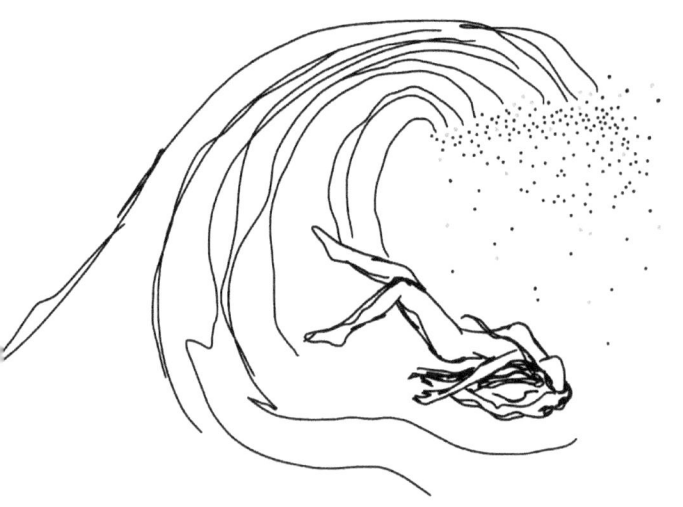

Whitney Popa

She pulled the covers
over her head,
trying to escape it.

A Wave Called Grief

"Who are you,
and why are you here?"
she cried.

As it swept back toward the horizon,
it replied.

Whitney Popa

"My name is Grief," it said.

A Wave Called Grief

Rattled, soaked, and sobbing,
she ran to the shower, where it hit her again.

She held out her hand, but it still washed over her,
leaving her crouched in the corner of the tub
with her arms wrapped around her legs,
chin on her knees.

Whitney Popa

A Wave Called Grief

All morning it crashed:
While she was doing her makeup,
sitting in traffic,
and trying to listen during meetings.

It took the taste out of her food,
the happy thoughts out of her head,
and the play out of her day.

Whitney Popa

Whenever she saw it coming,
she held up her hand to stop it.

Grief crashed into and washed over her anyway.

A Wave Called Grief

By evening, she was exhausted

Whitney Popa

and scared.

A Wave Called Grief

But then she had an idea.

She walked into a surf shop near her home and scanned the wall for the perfect board.

"That one," she told the shopkeeper, pointing to a white banana-shaped cruiser that shimmered as if it had been dusted with moonstone.

Whitney Popa

A Wave Called Grief

Whitney Popa

"A beauty," he nodded, taking it down.

While he went to the back to wax the board,
she looked around her.
She saw others evaluating their options,
their eyes wet like hers.

From the wave? she wondered.

A Wave Called Grief

At the cash register,
a man with salt and pepper hair and readers
signed his receipt.

To her right,
a young woman with freckles and a golden ponytail,
her hand clutched by a little boy with fluffy curls
and lights on his shoes,
tapped her foot impatiently.

Whitney Popa

On her left,
a cowboy lowered his hat
to shade his face.

A Wave Called Grief

The shopkeeper returned with her new board,
reflective and gleaming.
"You picked a good one," he said, handing it over.

"Now go shred!"

Whitney Popa

She smiled weakly, paid,
and opened the door to leave.

A Wave Called Grief

In front of her roared the ocean,
its waves crashing and retreating.

She turned toward it,
her board under her arm.

Whitney Popa

A Wave Called Grief

Her heart raced as she walked down the beach,
closer to the swells.
She knew Grief was in there.

Whitney Popa

"Come and get me!" she hollered.

A Wave Called Grief

And it did.
The water surged and rolled,
rising up to touch the sky.

She waited.

Whitney Popa

Grief barreled toward her.

This time, she didn't put up her hand.
Moving her board in front of her body,
she dropped onto it, paddling with cupped hands,
the water swirling around them.

A Wave Called Grief

The wave crested over her,
and she pushed the nose of her board down
to swim under it,
popping up to catch a sun ray

shining on her face.

Whitney Popa

A Wave Called Grief

She took a deep breath.

Water dripped down her eyes
to her cheeks
and onto her mouth.

Whitney Popa

She exhaled,
licking the salt from her lips.

A Wave Called Grief

She stood.

And she rode.

Whitney Popa

Whitney Popa

About the Author

Whitney Popa is a lot of things: a writer,
a cat herder, a wife, a mom, a friend.
She lives by the beach in Edmonds, WA.

@whitpopa   @ourwestpress

About the Illustrator

AnnaMarie is the founder of West Finch, a
design studio with a passion for books and
mental health. She currently calls Colorado
home alongside her cat, Daisy.

@westfinchstudio   westfinch.com

www.ingramcontent.com/pod-product-compliance
Lightning Source LLC
LaVergne TN
LVHW021120080426
835510LV00012B/1778